HARNESSING CUSTOMERS—
HOW TO INCREASE IMPULSE SHOPPING
IN SUPERMARKETS

HARNESSING CUSTOMERS— HOW TO INCREASE IMPULSE SHOPPING IN SUPERMARKETS

▼

A Thesis by Zeeshan-ul-hassan Usmani

iUniverse, Inc.

New York Lincoln Shanghai

Harnessing Customers—How to Increase Impulse
Shopping in Supermarkets

Copyright © 2007 by Zeeshan-ul-hassan Usmani

iUniverse books may be ordered through booksellers or by contacting:

iUniverse
2021 Pine Lake Road, Suite 100
Lincoln, NE 68512
www.iuniverse.com
1-800-Authors (1-800-288-4677)

ISBN-13: 978-0-595-43848-8 (pbk)
ISBN-13: 978-0-595-88173-4 (ebk)
ISBN-10: 0-595-43848-2 (pbk)
ISBN-10: 0-595-88173-4 (ebk)

Printed in the United States of America

A thesis
Submitted to Florida Institute of Technology
in partial fulfillment of the requirements
for the degree of

Master of Science
in
Computer Science

Melbourne, Florida
August, 2006

To my father Sardar-ul-hassan Usmani, who is always praying for my success thousands of miles away back home, without knowing what I am doing or what computer science is.

~Zeeshan-ul-hassan Usmani

THESIS COMMITTEE

Ronaldo Menezes, Ph.D.
Associate Professor and Thesis Advisor,
Department of Computer Science

Walter P. Bond, Ph.D.
Associate Professor,
Department of Computer Science

Muzaffar A. Shaikh, Ph.D.
Professor and Department Head,
Department of Engineering Systems

William D. Shoaff
Associate Professor and Department Head,
Department of Computer Sciences

PREAMBLE

Millions of dollars are spent every year on the understanding of customer behavior. In a capitalist society where competition is the norm, retails stores have to always stay on the edge of marketing and customer behavior research. The difficulty in understanding customers is not surprising—people are unpredictable and behave based on many influences.

But influence is the key in today's market. Stores make use of many "tricks" to influence customers in buying more products—fidelity cards, incremental discounts, last minute offers, and rebates are just a few examples. These approaches work because it is a known fact that humans are impulsive creatures and easily influenced. In fact, it may be argued that in a nature vs. nurture debate, influence is more linked to the later than the former. Children are greatly influenced by their parents and friends. Successful co-workers are a source of inspiration to the other workers in a company. Indeed, this can be better seen from an imitation standpoint; it is not really that influence is taking place, but rather that people tend to imitate what others do if they believe their payoff (in imitating) is high. In retail this is not different; the herding concept in marketing is well known and studied.

In this work, Zeeshan sets out to study the herding effect in supermarket and retail-store settings and the effect of technology to herding. He explores the possibility that an alternative sales model can be used to influence customer impulse purchasing while providing a valuable service to the customers themselves. Customers get to know about the shopping activities of others (in real time) and respond to these activities. Far from being the answer to all questions in the field, this work provides us with just some of the answers but, more importantly, it naturally opens our eyes to the possibilities that the herding theory can offer.

This work has attracted the attention of many important publications such as the Economist and the MIT Technology Review. If you are interested in the field of customer behavior and its relationship to technology, you should find this work a valuable document to help your research. If on the other hand, you are just curious about the future of supermarkets, the thesis should provide you with just a hint of what is to come, and how technology will be able to improve your life as a customer while also helping stores in their quest for being competitive.

Ronaldo Menezes
Associate Professor of Computer Sciences
Florida Institute of Technology

ABSTRACT

A Swarm-based Model for Increasing Impulse Shopping in Supermarkets

by

Zeeshan-ul-hassan Usmani

Thesis Advisor: Ronaldo Menezes, Ph.D.

In today's supermarket multi-billion dollar industry, impulse shopping accounts for 2 out of 3 purchases. The phenomenon is so prominent that some consider high levels of it to be a disorder in the same group as *Pyromania* (the impulse to burn things) and *Kleptomania* (the impulse to steal). Despite the current situation, most retail stores attempt to benefit from the fact that people are impulsive in nature as a way to maximize their profits. In order to improve on current levels of sales, retail stores and supermarkets need to look at out-of-the-box to solutions that may, at first, not appear useful. One such approach is the study of levels of self-organization in people *while they are doing their shopping*. This thesis discusses the status-quo of supermarket optimization and leaps into how a supermarket simulation can use real-time information about customer purchases. And apply models inspired in swarm intelligence to empower customers with products' sales level leading to an increase in impulse purchases.

CONTENTS

LIST OF FIGURES

LIST OF TABLES

LIST OF ABBREVIATIONS

ANN	Artificial Neural Networks
EDLP	Every Day Low Prices
EPC	Electronic Product Code
GA	Genetic Algorithm
GPS	Global Positioning System
KBS	Knowledge Base Systems
KNN	K-Nearest Neighbor
RFID	Radio Frequency IDentification
SKU	Stock Keeping Units
SWARM-MOVES	A simulation to test the proposed models
SWARM-SALES MODEL	A model based on customers' purchase information
SALES-MODEL	A model based on promotion depth (sales price) of the product

ACKNOWLEDGMENTS

In the name of Allah, the most beneficent and the most merciful, to Him is due all praise. I thank Him for enabling me to accomplish this research and put this work together.

> "I submit that if a man has not discovered something that he will die for, he is not fit to live."
>
> ~Martin Luther King, Jr.

I am Indebted to a number of persons who provided remarkable help to explore, understand, and code the proposed models and simulation. Some are more important than others, not because of their education or social status, but because they helped me at the right time, at the right place, and with the right kind of guidance.

Fulbright program deserves my special and sincere gratitude for the comprehensive support to my travel to the US and entire academic undertaking at Florida Tech. I am very grateful to Dr. Ronaldo Menezes and Professor William Shoaff for their wonderful academic advising. Dr. Menezes has an extra-ordinary sense to judge the time required for a particular task, which made my life horrible during the thesis. But, finally I am glad to be his student.

Many thanks also go to the thesis committee members, Dr. Walter Pat Bond and Dr. Muzaffar Shaikh for their invaluable comments. I would also like to offer my appreciation to Ms Penny Bernard for proofreading and editing the manuscript.

Finally, I became the "Faran Kaalified" as it refers to "Foreign Qualified" in my home town.

Thank you very much my RAB.

Zeeshan-ul-hassan Usmani
zeeshan_ul_hassan@yahoo.com

CHAPTER I

▼

INTRODUCTION

In today's supermarket multi-billion dollar industry, impulse shopping accounts for every 2 out of 3 purchases [Bangoli 1987]. Impulse shopping is an unplanned, immediate urge to buy something [Stern 1962]. Still, it is thought that improvement in impulse shopping is possible if customers are provided with more information about sales—such as what other customers are buying. Such an approach needs to encompass a new understanding of customers' shopping behavior and its effect on their purchase levels.

People generally follow the opinion of the majority—referred as *mob-mentality* in social sciences [Rosen 2002]. A person observing others performing a task is inclined to "join in" and perform the same task. The same is true in sales: the spread of information about a particular deal (i.e. products going on sale) from person to person may be an interesting sales tool. If many people refer to the price of a product as being a "good deal," people are inclined to believe and be led to buy the product in question.

This thesis introduces a model whereby customers become aware of other customers real-time shopping behavior and may hence be influenced by their purchases and the levels of purchases. This model is orthogonal to a sales model (where depth of price promotion increases the sales volume), but this thesis argues that it can have similar effects: increase in the overall shopping volume.

Recently, we have witnessed a rebirth toward the understanding of complex systems. The self-organizing models are one of the tools argued as appropriate to explain and study complexity. Self-organization is a phenomenon that refers to an increasing process of organization of a system without being directed by outside forces. From the point of view of supermarket sales, it is not hard to show that the analysis of customers' activities (movement, shopping behavior, etc.), while inside the supermarket, falls in the category of a complex system. One needs to look at only a few examples: *(i)* customers act independently of each other while in the supermarket—the path they take nor the products they buy is directed by the supermarket; *(ii)* the level of sales of products is an emergent value dependent upon customers' buying power that day, the level of discount for the product, the location of the product in the supermarket, and many others; *(iii)* external factors such as weather and natural disasters can drive behavior in sales that is hard to predict. All in all, there are many studies to understand and forecast customer behavior and some of them have achieved success, particularly during known commemorative dates such as Independence Day, Christmas, Halloween, etc. In any case, it is undeniable that an exact prediction (even on these holidays) is hard to be achieved.

Furthermore, their overall behavioral pattern is characterized as a self-organizing system, given that there is no centralized control (customers are not being directed in their purchases), the presence of feedback through the proposed model (what others are buying), and customer-to-product multiple interactions (customers' movement in aisles). Within this self-organized and seemingly distributed setting, what do exist are clues which make customers spend more and more often (e.g. special offers, mark-downs, campaigns). A missing and important clue to customers relates to the real-time purchase level of products—if a product is selling well, it is most likely a good deal or it is an important purchase due to some event (e.g. water during a hurricane watch/warning).

This thesis discusses current approaches to help supermarkets to achieve more sales volume, make more profit, and to provide additional information to customers that will help them to make better decisions by proposing the use of information emerging from real-time customer activities within the supermarket as another clue/information that can be used to be offered to in-store customers. Today's technology can easily enable this information to be fed to all customers in real-time. Examples of such technology via the use of RFIDs (Radio Frequency Identification) and intelligent carts are already in place in many experimental supermarkets, such as TESCO retail stores in UK and Metro experimental future-marts [Berthiaume 2004]. *Swarm-Moves* simulation shows that a model considering the information of what in-store customers are buying is likely to increase the volume of sales for products that are already selling well—what is selling well should continue to sell well.

This research looks at the self-organizing characteristics of a model (based on the information of what in-store customers buy) discusses current approaches to help supermarkets achieve more sales and profit, and proposes the use of strategies based on self-organization (in particular Swarm Intelligence) as the basis of a system that helps in the decision making process of customer to buy more on impulse. *Swarm-Moves* provides a simulation of a model where all customers in the store have their idea of what is on sale or is a so-called *good value*, based on the average shopping behavior of other customers in the store.

The proposed model uses only information about customers while they are in the store—after leaving the store, their in-store behavior is no longer considered. This work argues that this occurs due to reinforcement learning, where this reinforcement is useful to try to convince the customers to buy more, thus maximizing the store sales.

1.1   Motivation

What do the current and coming technologies hold for us to optimize supermarkets (increase sales and profit)? How can we feed more information to customers to improve their shopping experience? How can this information help them in their buying decisions? How can this whole process improve sales in supermarket? How do we know the most "commonly sold" product without having to revert to offline analysis? What is the relationship between promotion depth and sales volume? And how can a supermarket take advantage of the benefits of new technology in real-time? These are the questions that caused enough motivation to start this work. The reader will find the discussions of finding the answers to these questions in the following chapters.

1.2   Organization of Thesis

The thesis starts with this introductory chapter that gives an overall introduction about the topic of the thesis and the main motivations behind the research.

Chapter 2 provides literature review which contains a brief definition of Swarm Intelligence, an overview of a supermarket's past, present and future—(i.e. technologies, mechanisms, and requirements), and defines and typifies impulse shopping.

Chapter 3 discusses the new *sales model,* which incorporates impulse shopping, its explanation, and the applicable equation. This is followed by a discussion of the idea of *Swarm-Sales* model. This chapter also introduces the *Swarm-Sales model*-a novel approach (and simulation) based on the idea of Swarm Intelligence in order to increase sales. This would be accomplished by considering and tracking how customers are drawn to buy products impulsively—this approach has never been seen in the marketing and simulation literature. This chapter also discuses the factors that make the simulation such as a virtual supermarket and its design, the store configuration, the number of items in the store with their profiles (i.e. price, size, color, brand etc), the customers' profiles (i.e. like-dislike, available amount for shopping, preferences, etc), and impulse criteria. Chapter 3 also discusses the *Swarm-Sales* model for impulse reinforcement, the test data used to run the program, and the programming assumptions made about the supermarket being simulated.

Chapter 4 explains the results and the criteria being used in sample runs to evaluate the effects of the *Swarm-Sales* model on the customers' shopping behavior. This chapter contains charts that demonstrate the performance (the purpose is to achieve more sales and profit for the store) of *Swarm-Sales model* based on comparison with other models.

This thesis ends in Chapter 6 with the conclusion and suggestions for future work in this area.

CHAPTER 2

▼

LITERATURE REVIEW

This chapter will give the reader information about Swarm Intelligence, super-markets, impulse shopping, and why it is an important factor to increase sales.

2.1   Swarm Intelligence

Swarm Intelligence (SI) is normally used to refer to techniques that are inspired by social insects' behavior. Swarm intelligence systems are usually made up of numer-ous agents interacting with each other and with their environment. These interac-tions often lead to emergent behavior without any centralized control (no one is directing how the individuals should behave). Examples of such systems can be eas-ily found in nature, e.g. bird flocks, termite mounds, wolf packs, fish schools, bee hives and ant colonies, to name but a few. Social insects such as ants, bees, and wasps are unique in the way individuals cooperate to accomplish complex tasks. Each individual, by simply following a small set of rules and being influenced by locally available information is organized as a group in an emergent process that can accomplish the solution of many complex tasks. More importantly, the emergent solution could not be achieved by any individual in isolation—the whole is more than the sum of its parts (the individuals) [Bonabeau 1999].

A system based on Swarm Intelligence can solve complex tasks by integrating simple individual behavior in a decentralized society where individuals relinquish individualism for the wellbeing of the society. A change in the environment may change the results of the system and any change in the behavior of an individual may influence the behavior of the system.

Bonabeau *et al.* have described four principles that characterize a system based on Swarm Intelligence [Bonabeau 1999]:

- **Positive feedback:** reinforces good solutions present in the system, it ensures that over time population should stabilize around the best solution. Positive feedback is an event causing results in a greater chance of the same event happening again. For example, the customers are buying a 'good deal' and sending their feedback to *Swarm-Sales model* thus encouraging other customers to buy the same. It is the reinforcement of popular actions made by the customers.

- **Negative feedback:** minimizes the chances of getting bad solutions and avoid the premature convergence. It allows diversion from the 'known' solution over time. Negative feedback is an event causing results in a lesser chance of the same event happening again. For example, if nobody bought a previously known 'good deal' for few hours, it will be demoted by negative (or not good) feedback from the customers, say a product is bought by 1% of customers will not have the same effects as a product which is bought by 80% of the customers.

- **Randomness:** helps to explore creative and unconventional solutions. Randomness is also beneficial to avoid the side effects of positive feedback, where positive feedback can pronounce the small happenings in the system incase of few agents. Randomness is not an error in Swarm Intelligence systems, rather it acts as a way to explore and discover new solutions.

- **Multiple Interactions:** make the flow of information and data throughout the network or trail. It is necessary to adopt a new pattern. For example, customers are communicating their purchases to others by *Swarm-Sales model.*

According to Bonabeau and Meyer [Bonabeau 2001], the advantages of Swarm Intelligence are:

- **Flexibility:** the group can be compatible in a dynamic environment

- **Robustness:** irrespective of individual misbehavior or loss, the group can accomplish its tasks, and

- **Self-organization:** Inherent parallelism or distributed action with little or no supervision.

Swarm Intelligence is close to nature and studies the collective behavior of agents interacting with their environment, causing complex spatio-temporal patterns to emerge. For example, it is more natural to describe how shoppers move in a supermarket than to come up with the mathematical equations that govern the dynamics of the density of shoppers [Bonabeau 2002]. Moreover, Swarm Intelligence systems are easy to code because of the simplicity of their rules.

Emergence (an integral part of swarm-based systems) is the process of complex pattern formation from simple rules. It is the results of interactions at individual levels. For example, a traffic jam is the emergent result of interactions among many drivers, who (on an individual level) are trying to reach a destination fast or slow and thus following or breaking some legal, ethical, or moral rules, yielding the collective behavior of a traffic jam. This is an entirely distinct activity. Emergent behavior is generally unpredictable from lower-level descriptions. At the lowest-level, an emergent phenomenon either does not exist or is hard to see.

2.2   Supermarkets

Early grocery stores could have been called 'do not touch stores,' because customers could not touch the products. The customers had to order the items from one side of the counter while a sales person on the other side complete the order. The labor cost is huge for these stores. To cut the labor cost, retailers started trusting the customers and the idea of supermarkets came into existence. Since their debut in 1920's with Piggly-Wiggly stores [Supermarket 2003], supermarkets have been facing constant changes, innovations, and progress.

Nowadays, a typical supermarket holds more than 45,000 products and an average shopper visits a supermarket 2.2 times a week [Xavier 1994]. The supermarket industry—with more than 160 registered chains only in the United States—has a budget comparable to the budget of half of the countries in the world combined [Supermarket 2003]. Collectively, all of the supermarkets GDP (Gross Domestic Product) is top 20 in the world and its stock value has increased by 300% over the last decade. There are 200 million customers per week in the US alone who visits the supermarkets.

For instance, to show the size and the worth of supermarkets, *Wal-Mart* alone has 1.3 million employees (the largest private employer in the US), 4,300 stores worldwide, 250+ billion dollars annual sales, and 1.52 billion dollars a day record sales [Supermarket 2003, Lee 2004]. Wal-Mart is the largest corporation, grocer, and retailer in the world; currently, it accounts for 35% of all drug and food sales in the United States.

These all-in-one places have many constraints that arise from different perspectives. Whether it is the customers' shopping list (supermarket needs to keep almost every possible item of the customers' shopping list to satisfy the requirements), the positioning of the products, the launching of the new products, or even the retailers' greedy desire for more profit and sales, the truth is that supermarkets have to satisfy all stakeholders.

Researchers and managers have been working to improve the share (i.e. profit, sales volume, etc) and demands of all stakeholders for the last eight decades; the difficulty arises from the fact that these stakeholders have almost opposite needs [AWM 2005]. Retailers want to keep the customers in the store premises as long as possible to maximize sales and impulse purchases. On the other hand, most customers want to leave the supermarket as soon as possible—most likely when they purchase their planned shopping items [Bucklin 2001].

Research has been done to figure out the ways to keep the customer longer in stores, such as internet booths, cafes, reading zones, saloons, ATM machines, and drug stores [Smith 1989]. Customers want value for their money and retailers want maximum sales and profit. There is always a tension between these two factors—should one favor the customers or the retailer when designing and setting supermarkets [Larson 2004]?

Today, supermarkets are a theater, where the characters are non-living objects. They have to act, communicate with customers, convey their benefits, re-route, and influence the customers for more sales without the ability to talk and convince. In this theater, there are different colored lights for different characters (products). There are lights to give a life to seafood and to make pizza look tastier. There are sounds to increase the sales of Rock-n-Roll music and set the overall flow of the supermarket [Morrison 1999]. A typical supermarket needs the service of designers, colorists, calligrapher, architect, artists, lighting specialists, brand managers, image marketers, logistic managers, and many others.

2.2.1   Trends in Supermarket Optimization

Every supermarket has the increase of profit and sales as their main priority. The more profit and sales volume, the more likely it is that a store will survive.

There are generally two ways to achieve an increase of profit and sales volume: *out-store* and *in-store* tactics [Vornberger 1997, Xavier 1994]. Out-store tactics deals with supply-chain management, personnel management, inventory management, advertising campaigns, marketing, product positioning, pricing and all other similar activities dealing with the manufacturing of the product to the placement of the products on the supermarket shelves. Out-store tactics generally deal with operational costs and procedures. In-store tactics look at how to increase profit and sales using mechanisms that take place inside the store. Known tactics include (but are not limited to): bargains, everyday low prices, special and limited offers, buy-one-get-one offers, free samples, shelf-reorganization, cross categorization, and use of previous data to forecast the sales and requirements for the future [Vornberger 1997, Xavier 1994].

Retailers can increase profit either by decreasing costs or increasing sales. Cost reduction is generally based on the operational level (e.g. personnel management, stock management, use of technology, etc.), while the increase of sales could be based on out-store or in-store tactics, or a combination of both processes.

Several in-store factors influence the purchase of a product, whether it is a planned purchase or not. In-store factors survived the customers' decision process inside the store; these include knowledge of the store, available time for shopping, special offers, promotions, atmosphere, and customer mood [Danziger 2004].

This thesis is not intended to look at out-store tactics to increase profit and volume of sales. This is not the focus of this research; however, a few papers on out-store tactics have been reviewed in this thesis to make the differences between out-store and in-store clearer.

The time frame for the collected papers dealing with in-store tactics for supermarket optimization is from 1970 to 2004. The criterion to select the papers is based on their relevance to in-store tactics and the proposed work. There was only one paper chosen for any particular subject—if there are several papers discussing how Genetic Algorithms can be used to improve marketing strategies, this thesis will mention only one (generally the most recent) to make a comparison.

Table 2.1 provides an overview of previous research in supermarket optimization. The table is organized with seven columns: who did the work; what has been done, that is, what was the purpose of the research; whether it falls in the out-store or in-store category; whether it is work that affects sales and/or profit in real-time; whether there is an indication of the consideration of *impulse* shopping to increase sales; and whether shelf reorganization is used to accomplish the purpose, i.e. increasing sales.

Who	What	Out-Store	In-Store	Real-Time	Impulse	Shelf
[Larson 2004]	Shopping Paths		✓	No	No	Yes
[Vornberger 1997,Vornberger 1994]	Neural Networks for Future Sales		✓	No	No	No
[Xavier 1994]	Shelf-Management and Space Elasticity		✓	No	No	Yes
[Marks 1998]	Genetic Algorithm for Marketing	✓		No	No	No
[Dologite 1993]	KBS for Product Positioning		✓	No	No	Yes
[Jhonson 2004]	Demand and Supply Chain Management	✓		No	No	No
[Lindo 2005]	Optimization is Sales and Marketing	✓		No	No	Yes
[Neilson 1992]	KBS for Market Analysis	✓		No	No	No
[Supermarket 2003, Rousseeuw 2005]	Data Mining		✓	No	No	No
[Bucklin 2001]	Expenditure Decisions		✓	No	Yes	No
[Naert 1988]	Shelf Allocation		✓	No	No	Yes
[Smith 1989]	Store Environment and Available Time		✓	No	Yes	No
[Costjens 1981]	Optimization of Retail Space		✓	No	No	Yes
[Cox 1970, Curhan 1972, Williamson 1999]	Shelf-Space and Unit Sales		✓	No	No	Yes
[UIE 2001]	Factors of Impulse Purchases		✓	No	Yes	No
[Hoch 1989]	Customers' Learning from Experience		✓	No	No	No
[Jacoby 2002]	Modeling Stimulus-Organism-Response		✓	No	No	No
[Milliman 1982, Morrison 1999]	Effect of Background Music		✓	Yes	No	No

Who	What	Out-Store	In-Store	Real-Time	Impulse	Shelf
[Reinhold 1983]	Store Ergonomics		✓	No	No	Yes
[Sommer 1982]	Mental Mapping of Supermarkets		✓	No	No	Yes
[Stern 1962]	Impulse Buying Factors		✓	No	Yes	No

Table 2.1: Trends in Supermarket Optimization

The majority of the research has concentrated on the use of neural networks [Vornberger 1994], genetic algorithms [Marks 1998], KDD (Knowledge Discovery in Databases) and data mining [Dologite 1993, Jhonson 2004] to search the patterns and information in the past data to predict the future sales and requirements. For example, a neural network is trained to predict the future values of a time series that consists of the weekly demand on items in a super-market. Genetic algorithms are used to find out the most competitive marketing strategy for product positioning by creating the population of all available strate-gies and taking out the best after evolution, based on some *goodness* criteria.

[Jacoby 2002] looks at another dimension of shopping behavior. He explained a model of 'history associated with particular product' in human mind as drive-cue-response-experience-consequence-resultant model. He demonstrated it with the help of human psychology. When a customer sees the product, it triggers the customers' past experience followed by a response (good or bad), which con-tributes to making a decision about buying the product. He argues that regardless of what marketing tools, brands, or means of advertisement are in-place, the cus-tomer's first response comes from past experience, whether it is his/her own or given by someone else.

[Smith 1989]. discussed the effects of *available time for shopping* and *store knowledge* (i.e. familiar store—information about aisles and the products they carries) on purchasing and customers' behavior. *Smith* also discussed *store knowl-edge* as one of the prime factors to increase impulse shopping. One can work on this factor by providing store maps and floor layouts to the customers, *this* work is intended to pass information related to products as a feedback to increase impulse shopping and not considering the other factors which are related to store, like layouts, decoration, music, lights, and category arrangements.

[Larson 2004] talked about the customers' shopping paths to find out the clusters and canonical trips (general common paths). The main goal of this research was to know the densely populated paths and low traffic paths to place the products accordingly. Based on cluster information of products and the resultant canonical trips of customers, this work also suggests the supermarket organization for future customers to make more and simplified clusters that will reduce congestions and save the overall time to shop in the supermarkets.

[Sommer 1982] applied commonly used technique in geography and psychology called 'mental mapping' to know the cognitive orientation of customers within supermarkets. This work has shown that a product placed on side aisles can easily be recalled instead of a product on central aisles. This work seconds the findings of [Larson 2004] where side paths are densely populated as compared to central paths.

[Curhan 1972] investigated the relationship between shelf space and unit sales. He found that there is a very little relationship between these two and that the volume of sales is more dependent upon other factors, like price and product characteristics.

As you can see in Table 2.1, there is only one incident where the possibility of real-time increase in sales has been discussed, but it does not include impulse shopping as a factor to increase sales [Milliman 1982, Morrison 1999]. None of the work has discussed the possibility of a real-time increase in sales and profits based on impulse shopping parameters; this is what this thesis proposes through the use of a model and simulation called *swarm-moves*. [Milliman 1982] realized the need to influence the customers in real-time. He used background music to create certain attitudes among employees and customers in order to stimulate customers' purchasing, to portray the supermarket image, to reduce the work pressure, and to set the overall shopping flow.

The human factors department of Kodak Inc. has done a marvelous work in special purpose lightning in supermarkets [Reinhold 1983]. They have made recommendations for lightning at surface level, lights for plastic or glass items, fluorescent lights, polarized lights, brightness patterns, cross-polarization, diffuse reflections, and trans-illuminations. The goal for this work is to find out the best set of lights with suitable color and voltage which makes the product looks good. For example, brightness patterns enhance the look of jewelry; fluorescent lights make apparel more fancy, and polarized lights to make the produce look fresh.

The use of music and lights are good examples of influencing customers in real-time to affect their shopping behavior and to find out the optimum set of music, lights, and shelf organization for a particular group of customers. Although this could be a good direction for future work, this is not addressed in this *thesis*.

We argue that study of emergent buying behavior of customers in a store can be used in conjunction with other techniques, such as music, lights, shelf organization, and product positioning for particular group of customer in a given time. In fact, it may even be possible to later use variations of the model described here to aid the decision about music, light, and others.

The majority of these and other consulted research [Rousseeuw 2005, Rheingold 2002, Zaltman 2003] either work before customer gets into the market (out-store tactics) or after customer leaves the market (in-store tactics: bargain prices, KDD, and data mining for future customers) based on recent customers' purchases and behavior.

The *Swarm-Sales model* is focused on in-store customers, those who are already in the supermarket, busy doing their shopping. It attempts to deal with how one can stretch the customers' buying limits and what the store can offer to them in real-time. Ideally, the implementation of our model can provide customers with a better shopping experience and retailers with a higher sales level, thus easing the tension that we described earlier between the customers' and the stores' goals.

Presently, supermarkets influence the way we live and shop; they also reflect our cultures. The future holds revolutionary innovations and changes for supermarkets like RFID, smart shelves, self-checkouts, electronic product code (for automated labeling by manufacturers), every day low prices (recommended by advance supply chain management tools), and knowledge based inventory management tools [Supermarket 2003]. We have to look differently to gain the advantages offered by these innovations to increase profit and sales.

2.3   Impulse Shopping

Impulse shopping is an immediate, unintended, powerful, and persistent urge to buy a product [Zaltman 2003]. Generally speaking, impulse buying is defined as unplanned buying, that is any purchase not planned in advance [Stern 1962].

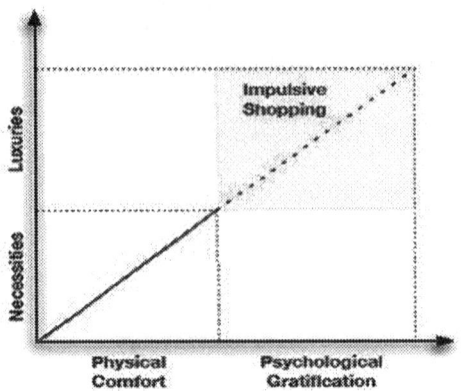

Figure 2.1: Impulse Shopping

Generally speaking, necessities of life, like food, clothing, and house items fall into the category of planned shopping, whereas items that account for psychological gratification, such as music CDs, DVDs, and jewelry, falls into the category of impulse shopping. In Figure 2.1, we can observe that as we move on the x-axis from physical comfort to physiological gratification, the products (in the y-axis) move from necessities to superfluous products. Clearly there are exceptions to the rule—as a person can buy an extra jacket on impulse, he can also buy an Xbox as a planned item.

Impulse shopping is more like what we want as compared to what we need. Sometimes customers buy an item just for the feeling of items being owned without any specific reason [Danziger 2004]. As a general rule, it is very hard to know what causes a person to buy on impulse, or at least it is hard to have a reason that can be generalized to most people.

2.3.1   Types of Impulse Shopping

Stern described four types of impulse shopping as follows [Stern 1962]:

- *Pure Impulse:* Unplanned and immediate urge to buy a product that breaks the normal shopping pattern.

- *Reminder Impulse:* Shopper sees an item or an advertisement about that product and remembers that he/she is out of stock.

- *Suggestion Impulse:* Customer has no prior experience of an item, but he/she sees the item and realizes the need for it.

- *Planned Impulse:* Customer want to buy some product just because it is on sale or it gives the impression for being a bargain.

Authors categorize impulse shopping differently based on consumer behavior, marketing strategies, social aspects, or on psychological roots of human beings [Newman 1999, Danziger 2004]. However, from the point of view of this dissertation, they all fall into the general description of 'unplanned shopping.' One can classify the information given by the proposed *Swarm-Sales* model as *suggested impulse* or *reminder impulse,* in other words, what others customers buy could be a suggestion or a reminder to buy a particular item. In either case, information provided by the *Swarm-Sales model* is a motivation for a customer to buy a product on impulse. One should note that every time a customer sees a product, he/she analyses a series of factors in order to decide whether to buy the product. Stores use these factors to their advantage, trying to improve the probability of a customer buying the product.

2.3.2   Factors that Influence Impulse Shopping

According to User Interface Engineering Corporation, the level sales offer and price are two main factors of impulse shopping [UIE 2001]. Stern extended this work to a more detailed number of factors; nine in total [Stern 1962]:

- *Low Price:* Customers are more attracted to products which are on sale or have introductory or special offers. Low price is always the most dominant factor to attract customers.

- *Marginal Need:* Customers see a product and feel the need for it, like a stationary item or cleaning material. This is one example where the impulse purchase does not normally fall in the category of a luxury item, an exception to the rule depicted in Figure 2.1.

- *Mass Distribution:* This is another interesting factor which influences the customers' decisions. Products are mass distributed in the store (normally for free) leading the customer to take the product home even though he/she did not plan to do so.

- *Advertisement:* Sometimes one sees an advertisement of an item on television or on a banner hanging in the front of the supermarket and becomes inclined to purchase that product. Sometimes we need it and sometimes we do not—advertisements incite our impulsive nature.

- *Prominent Display:* Stern also argues that prominent display can increase sales. When one sees a beautiful dress on a display wearing by a statue, its effect on the customer is greater than having the same dress on a shelf.

- *Short Product Life:* Research has shown that products that are short lived are regular impulse items, since there is minimal chance of a product being wasted. Tissue papers, gum, pain-killers, and chocolates are good examples of this.

- *Small Size and less weight:* This is another important factor of impulse shopping. People generally do not buy large, heavy products like a refrigerator or a car on impulse. The smaller and lighter the product is the larger the probability of a customer buying it on impulse.

- *Ease of Storage:* This is related to the above parameter. Research has shown that products that can be stored easily have more chance of being bought on impulse. People are reluctant to buy items on impulse which can not fit into their car trunk or house, such as a Christmas tree or poker table.

These nine factors can be used to influence in-store customers in real-time along with the *Swarm-Sales* model—as argued before, the proposed model is orthogonal to all other factors. In essence the proposed model could be seen as a 10th factor that drives impulse: knowledge of other customers' purchases. Retailers may want to exploit the information given by *Swarm-Sales model* as well as work on any of these 9 factors as a mechanism to influence customers (e.g. if a product x is bought by 80% of in-store customers, the manager may like to place it on *prominent displays*, reduce its *price*, or increase its *advertisement* to increase its sales even further).

2.3.3   Why Impulse is an Important Parameter for Supermarket Optimization?

Impulse shopping is one of the most important and least considered aspects of supermarket sales. It represents 66% of all the money spent on shopping [Bangoli 1987]. Impulse shopping is constantly increasing over the years mainly due to new sales tactics used by stores to attract customers and to keep them in the store.

Supermarket is a big catalog now, trends in supermarket optimization have shifted from planned listed items to unplanned shopping purchases because the customers can take advantage of sales, bargains, and special offers. People go to supermarkets with few items in mind, but they explore the items and sales. They make their choice in real-time based on the level of sales; the result is that they end up buying more products than planned.

Generally, customers like to shop at familiar stores where they are knowledgeable with the merchandise displays and store procedures. This familiarity gives them a feeling of control and encourages exploratory shopping—looking around and exploring what else is there in the supermarket. On the other hand, at a somewhat unfamiliar store, customers focus on finding what they need [Danziger 2004].

Although impulse shopping can be observed for any product, there are some that are more prominent. A 1987 study shows that 80% of buying decisions made in-store for candy, gum, snacks, pickles, relishes, pasta, cookies, crackers, and sauces are impulsive [Bangoli 1987]. However, stores can improve on these numbers for other products by providing the customers with more information related to products being purchased in real-time. The message is clear: customers need to be influenced, mostly while they are in the store. Once they leave, the power that the store can exercise over the customer diminishes greatly.

CHAPTER 3

▼

MODELS AND SIMULATION

As mentioned before, there are out-store tactics to get customers to visit the store. Once a customer selects and visits the store, the store's next concern is to make the customer buy products and possibly keep him/her in the store for a long time. In today's diverse, media-rich, info-driven, and heavily competitive marketplace, it is very hard to target customers with need-based advertising. What do customers really need? How can the masses be targeted if the needs of customers are as diverse as their backgrounds? Satisfying consumers' needs has less to do with the fulfillment of physical necessities and more to do with gratifying desires [Danziger 2004]. The act of buying, rather than the item being consumed, is more prominent in today's supermarkets and this makes it really hard to optimize supermarkets (for more sales and profits) in its fullest.

This work proposes a new way to increase the overall sales in the supermarkets by using the information of in-store customers' purchases and sending it back as feedback to other customers to motivate impulse shopping. To make a comparison in the simulation environment, the proposed *Swarm Sales Model* has been compared to the *Sales Model*—derived from the literature review of supermarket optimization (discussed in Chapter 2).

3.1 Sales Model

The *Swarm-Moves* simulation includes two models, one is a *sales model* where customers are influenced by discount (sales) price and the second is a *swarm sales model* where customers are influenced by the collective choice of other customers in the store. Both models include customer profiles (customers' likelihood/probability of buying an item from a particular category).

Everyone likes a bargain and *sales model* does not disregard this—price is one of the main factors to cause impulse buying [UIE 2001]. It has been argued that the influence of sales price or the depth of promotion usually results in spikes of sales volume [Garrick 1986]. It is observed that spikes in sales volume is not linearly proportional to promotion depth (price elasticity) being offered to that product [Dawes 2004, Nagle 1987, Edward 1995]. Equation 1 attempts to capture this behavior and be consistent with the observed data and previous experiments [Jedidi 1999, Duncan 2001, Supermarkets 2002, Cotton 1978].

The following *Sales Model* implements the *Price-Depth Vs Volume-Sales* relationship through Equation 1. In the equation, μ is a location parameter. a is a shape parameter, and x is the discount level being offered to the product. The values $\mu = 0.1$ and $a = 0.03$ have been used in this work after an empirical analysis to generate the consistent graph with the previous studies.

$$f_{onsale}(x) = 1 - e^{x\log(1-a)} - \mu \qquad (1)$$

The following graphs demonstrate the effect of different values of constants a (shape parameter) and μ (location parameter).

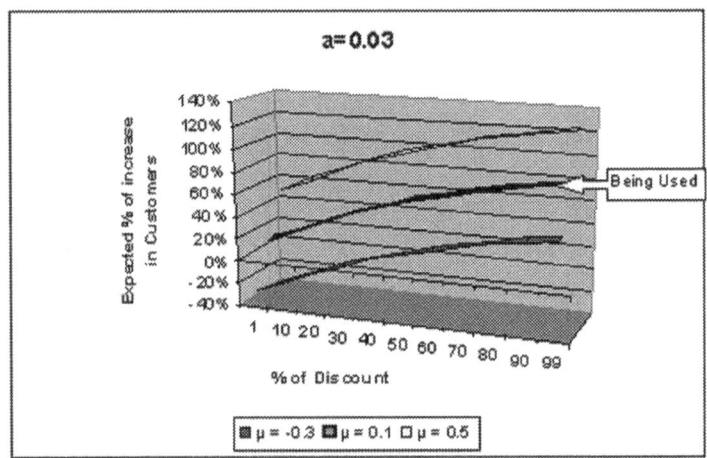

Figure 3.1: Different Values of Constant *μ* in *Sales-Model*

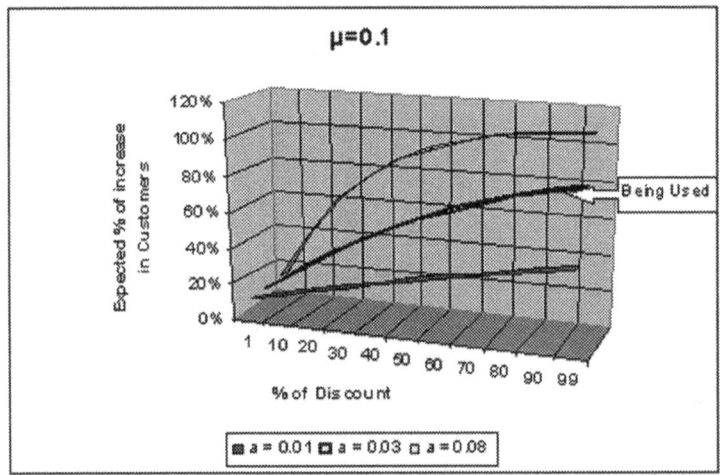

Figure 3.2: Different Values of Constant *a* in *Sales-Model*

This equation is used in *Sales Model* in conjunction with *customers' profile* (*likelihood*) of buying an item from the particular category. For instance, a customer has a 50% probability (likelihood) of buying a product in his *profile* and the product is on 30% off sale. This model will increase the probability of purchase of that product, while the level of increase in probability will be given by Equation 1 (the value of *x* is 30% here).

3.2   The Idea Behind Swarm-Sales

The influence upon and reinforcement of impulse shopping could be a good approach to increase sales in the supermarkets. Any model trying to increase impulse shopping should consider the behavior of in-store customers, such as the paths customers take and the items they buy. Past data and future predictions may not be good parameters to increase impulse shopping.

Generalization is a prime characteristic of out-store tactics, but it kills the individuality of the customers, thus minimizing the chances of impulse shopping. For instance, the marketing managers choose a product for marketing (e.g. to place it on sale, to promote it through mass advertisement or to place it on prominent display in the store) in the stores throughout the country. The criterion to choose the product is based on product's characteristics such as the number of units sold on average or the highest profit ever made by that product. Now, this product is marketed throughout the country. While this generalized form of customer influence may work, it is not tailored towards the individual's needs. It is possible that for a given product the total number of units sold is not uniformly distributed in the country-90% units sold only in California and 10% in the rest of the US. Also, a product may be selling well because of some local event in a particular area (i.e. plywood in hurricane-threatened areas)—not meaning that hardboards should be marketed in Arizona or some other states that are not being affected by hurricanes.

The proposed *Swarm-Sales model* in the next section is capable of promoting more local needs. A product which is bought by 90% of customers in a small store in Melbourne, Florida will be different from a product which is bought by another 90% of customers in the store of Santa Monica, California. Even more notably is that the model accounts for temporal changes—customers' needs may differ in different times of the day for the same store in the same day. The product sales level is different according to in-store customers; say majority of in-store customers are elderly in the morning and teens in the evenings.

This work proposes a supermarket optimization model (and its simulation) based on Swarm Intelligence to identify parameters and their values that can influence customers to buy more on impulse in a given period of time. In the proposed model, customers are assumed to have trolleys equipped with technology that can aid the passing of products' information directly from the store to them in real-time (i.e. RFID, Wi-Fi, etc.). Therefore, they can get the information about other customers purchase patterns and may be constantly informing the store of their own shopping behavior. This can be easily achieved because the trolleys "know" what products they contain at any point. The main premise of this model is that the combination of what all the customers are doing (the collective behavior inside the supermarket) can be used to indicate how good a particular deal in the store actually is—if many people are buying, it is probably a good deal.

Recommendations should be able to vary with time. Note that the recommendations are considering only in-store customers and the emergent behavior of one group may not necessary be fit for another group in a different day or time. We do not need to worry about why people buy and what are their ages, race, sex or financial status are to increase impulse shopping. All this information, although important, is embedded in their behavior and will be captured by *Swarm-Sales model*. If the average in-store customers are from mid-salary range class *Swarm-Sales model* will automatically detect this property from their purchases, and will be giving clues to other customers to purchase products within their price range.

It should be noted that by saying *Real-Time* the time window for customers' data is the current state of the supermarket (How many customers are there? What are their purchases? etc.). This time window can be programmed according to supermarket's need, for example, If a supermarket is not big enough to have hundreds of customers in few hours (thus recommendations may fluctuate intensely due to small number of customers in the supermarket), it may consider to redefine the time window for customers' data by incorporating last day statistics or last week or last month as a basis of recommendations to customers. For example, there is a small store with 10 or 20 customers at any time; the *Swarm-Moves Simulation* can be programmed to meet the requirements of this small store. When customers like to buy an item, they can have feedback of that item from last day, week or month (i.e.: 67% customers bought that product last week)

The proposed *Swarm-Sales model* captures the *collective average choice* that customers are taking. *Swarm-Moves* simulation implements a model where customers have profiles, and are influenced by the collective choice of other customers in the store.

For example, if 83% customers bought water, it may be difficult to find a reason behind it, but we are not interested to find this reason. We want to take advantage of this event by providing this information to other 17% customers in the supermarket who did not purchase the water. It could be because of coming hurricane, some unknown reason, a new episode of the Friends sitcom program, or advertisement. All we know is the fact: water is being sold at a higher rate. The model provides this information to other customers so that they are led to buy water on impulse.

We do not have to discuss why people buy. The important factor is that something is selling well. Whatever it is, it is the *collective average choice* of customers in store and we can try to sell the same items to others without knowing the reason. Other researchers discussed what is selling, what quantities, and what is the reason, so that they can plan the future. We want to explore the same parameters to plan the present—the next few hours or minutes. The main premise is *whatever is selling, pile it up and sell more*. The simulation presented in Chapter 4 was implemented to test the proposed model and the results presented in Chapter 5 are encouraging.

3.3   Swarm-Sales Model

The *Swarm-Sales Model* is based on customers' choice of product. The number of customers buying a particular product is used as a feedback to other customers by *Swarm-Sales Model* to increase the probability of that customer buying a product. The proposed model argues that the customers are not interested in others' purchases until the level reaches a threshold, from which point customers become heavily influenced by the purchase level. In other words, if few customers in a store are buying a product the increase on the probability of a particular customer who is receiving this information is small; on the other hand, if many customers are buying the product the increase on the probability is also large. Mathematically speaking, we used a sigmoid function (S-shaped) to convey the aforementioned. Figure 3.1 shows the expected behavior of *Swarm-Sales Model* with *customers' profile*.

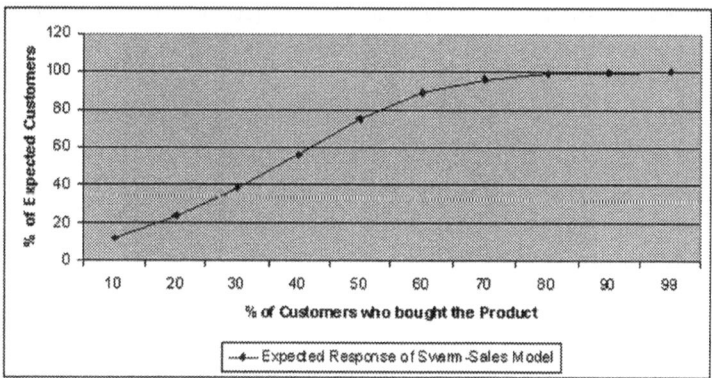

Figure 3.3: Expected Response of *Swarm-Sales* Model with Customers' Profile

The customers following a sigmoid-like behavior (spike after some threshold and stabilizes at the end) has been observed by many researchers in different fields. [Berger 2000] discussed the issue in consumer culture throughout the US, and in evolution of communication over-time. [Salzman 2003] had similar findings in his work of *power of influence and creates demand*. [Rosen 2002] discussed the similar behavior in terms of *viral marketing* and *invisible networks*. Since, there is no previous model available to test the customers' response on feedback of other customers' purchases; this thesis utilized a model that has been observed in other areas (as mentioned above).

The *Swarm-Sales Model* is formalized in Equation 2, where *x* represents the percentage of customers currently buying the product in supermarket. Constants *a* and *b* control the shape and the mid-point of the sigmoid function. The simulations were performed using *a* = 0.1 and *b* = ?50.

The value of *x* (percentage of customers currently buying the product) is given by the ratio of the number of trolleys containing that item (*ItemFrequency*) by the number of total trolleys in the supermarket (*TotalCustomers*). Note that it is assumed that all customers have a trolley; the trolleys that are not being used by a customer are not active and therefore not counted in *TotalCustomers*. It should also be noted that the program is counting only one instance if the item is present in customers' trolley regardless of the number of items the particular customer bought (or carries in his/her trolley). This simplification helps us to stop recommending an item which is bought by a single customer (many units) to others. For example, if 1 customer out of total 10 customers in the supermarket bought 7 units of item *A*, one cannot argue that this should have the same effect of the same item being purchased by 7 out of 10 customers in the supermarket. In the above model, the value of *x* for the item *A* will be only 10% in first case and 70% in the second case. It should be clear that by saying *bought* we mean the items present in the customers' trolleys and assuming that customers are going to buy them. If the customer decides to remove an item from his/her trolley the item will automatically be removed from the total count.

$$f_{swarm}(x) = \frac{1}{(1+\frac{1}{e^{a(x+b)}})} \tag{2}$$

Following graphs demonstrates the effect of different values of constants *a* (shape parameter) and *b* (mid-point of the sigmoid function) over the graph.

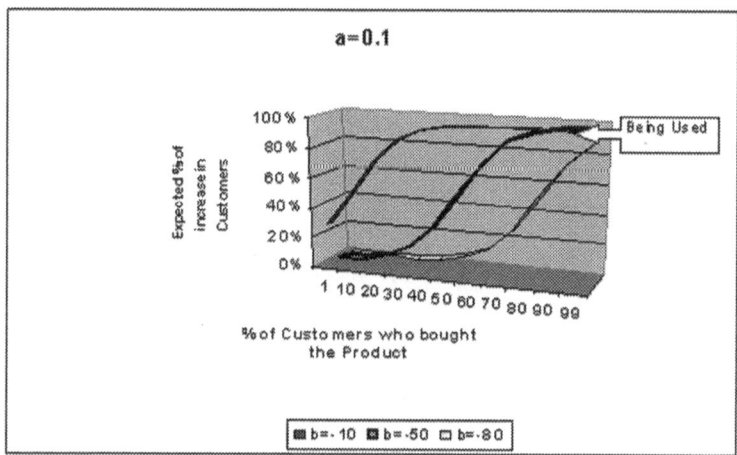

Figure 3.4: Different Values of constant b in *Swarm-Sales Model*

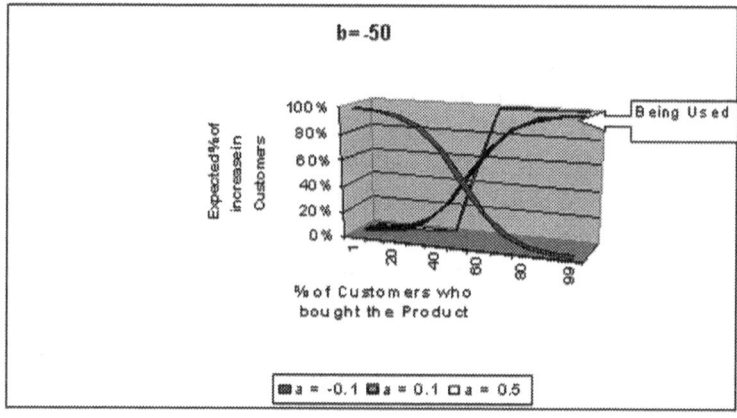

Figure 3.5: Different Values of constant *a* in *Swarm-Sales Model*

3.4   Coding

The implementation of *Swarm-Moves* simulation uses a database where profiles of customers and products are stored. The database contains 120 different products of twelve categories (users can give as many categories as they want):

Electronics, Produce, Pharmacy, Garments, Cosmetics, School, Bakery, Sports, CDs, Bed-N-Bath, Toys, and Miscellaneous.

In order to make the decision about buying an item on impulse, the program uses Equation 3 where a factor, *F(x)*, is applied to the *likelihood* probability of buying on impulse (from the customer profile), the factor *F(x)* represents the *Sales-Model* (in Equation 1), or the *Swarm-Sales Model* (in Equation 2), or both applied in series. The probability p_{new} is then used to decide whether the customer gets the product.

$$P_{new} = P_{profile} + (1 - P_{profile}) \times F(x) \qquad (3)$$

When a customer sees the product, the *likelihood* of buying that product comes from his/her personal profile. *New Probability (p_{new})* is the increased probability by *Sales-Model* or *Swarm-Sales model* or both in series. Then the program picks a random number between 0 and 1, if the number lies between 0 and the p_{new} (New Probability) customer will buy the product, otherwise he/she will not buy the product.

Let us consider a complete example. If one assume that the *likelihood* (probability) of buying a product as *P* and influencing *Factor* (sales-model or swarm-sales model) as *P'*. *P'* is an attractor for *P*, that will always increase the value of *P*. For example, if *P* is 0.4 and *P'* is 0.6, *P* will increase by some percent (given by the model being used) or if *P* is 0.6 and *P'* is 0.4, *P* will again increase by some percent (given by the model being used). The *P'* is the reinforcement being added to probability *P* to maximize the chances of purchase of a product on impulse. Overall, the *Factor* is influencing the impulse buying decision of the customer with positive feedback. Let us clarify the above mentioned description with a running example using actual values.   Customer's likelihood of buying a product (that is on 90% discount price) has increased from 50% to 89.80% in this example.

Likelihood ($P_{profile}$) $=$ 0.5 (50%)

Sales-Off % $=$ 0.90 (90%)

$$f_{onsale}(x) = 1 - e^{x \log(1-a)} - \mu$$

$$f_{onsale}(x) = 1 - e^{0.9 \log(1-0.03)} - 0.1$$

$$F(x) \quad = \quad 0.7959 \ (79.59\%)$$

$$P_{new} = P_{profile} + (1 - P_{profile}) \times F(x)$$

$$P_{new} \quad = \quad 0.5 + (1 - 0.5) \times 0.7959$$

$$P_{new} \quad = \quad 0.8980 \ (89.80\%)$$

Following tables demonstrate few examples of different likelihood (probabilities) coming from the customers' profiles to buy an item, product's Sales-Off percentage, the results given by *Sales-Model* and *Swarm-Sales Model* equations and the respective new probabilities to buy that product.

Likelihood (Profile %)	Sales-Off %	F(x) = Sales Model	P_{new}
10	10	22.391	30.152
20	20	33.246	46.597
30	30	42.756	59.929
40	40	51.088	70.653
50	50	58.388	79.194
60	60	64.783	85.913
70	70	70.386	91.116
80	80	75.294	95.059
90	90	79.594	97.959
99	99	83.007	99.830

Table 3.1: Example runs using *Sales-Model*

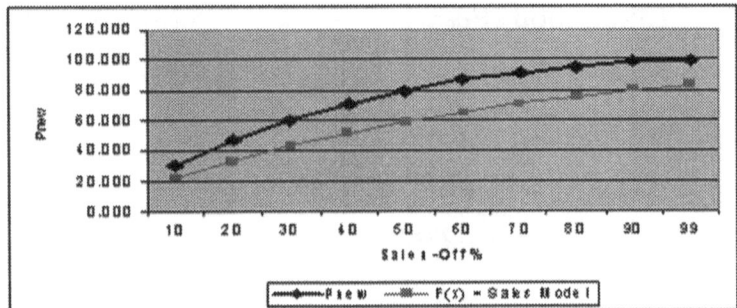

Figure 3.6: Behavior of Table 3.1 (Example runs using *Sales Model*)

Likelihood (Profile %)	% of Customers	F(x) = Swarm Sales	P_{new}
10	10	1.799	11.619
20	20	4.743	23.794
30	30	11.920	38.344
40	40	26.894	56.136
50	50	50.000	75.000
60	60	73.106	89.242
70	70	88.080	96.424
80	80	95.257	99.051
90	90	98.201	99.820
99	99	99.261	99.993

Table 3.2: Example runs using *Swarm-Sales Model*

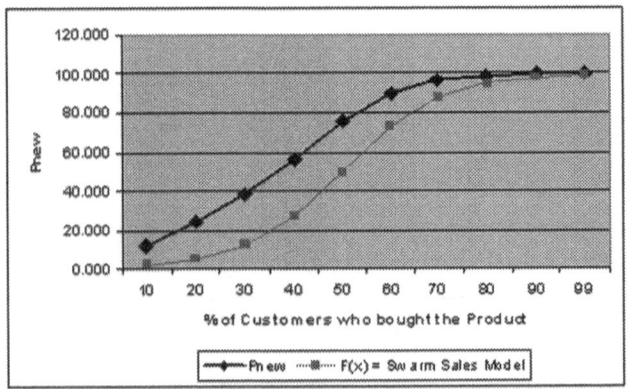

Figure 3.7: Behavior of Table 3.2 (Example runs using *Swarm-Sales Model*)

3.5   Swarm-Moves Simulation

The *Swarm-Moves* simulation is the virtual supermarket providing the visual display to run and test the proposed model. Swarm-Moves simulation is using two types of profiles: *Item profiles* and *Customer profiles* as described in later sections. There are three sections of the screen, as can be seen in Figure 3.8.

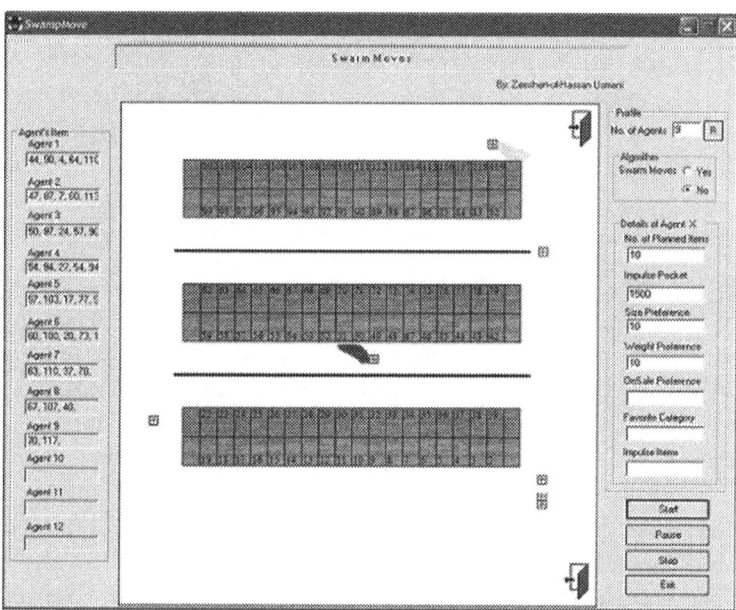

Figure 3.8: *Swarm-Moves Simulation Screen*

The right panel has the number of agents (customers) desired to be part of the simulation (supermarket); the range is between zero and twelve due to screen visual limitations. However it is possible to run the simulation with up to 500 agents without animating their movement in the screen. The algorithm box shows whether you are using *Swarm-Sales model* or not. The *Swarm-Sales model* is responsible for reinforcement to increase impulse shopping. Simulation without *Swarm-Sales model* will act as a normal supermarket with *Sales model* impulse behavior. The mid panel of right side shows the profile of selected agent (agent can be selected by clicking on agent's number at the left panel), and the start, pause, stop and exit buttons to play the simulation.

The left panel has agents' (customers) trolleys to record purchased items in real-time. These trolleys have all items, planned items and items bought on impulse. By clicking on trolley you can mark the moving agent (customer) and it will show in dark brown color (if present on the screen). Selecting a trolley number greater than total number of agents being selected for current simulation will do nothing. As soon as the simulation starts, the trolleys will have all the planned items. The simulation is using it as an initial condition so that these items (planned) can affect the impulse purchases.

The middle of the screen shows the layout of *Swarm-Moves*. There are 120 products of 12 categories (10 items of each category in sequential order), six tracks and six shelves. When the simulation starts, the agents enter the supermarket (starting from entrance door), the yellow lens shows the scanning of the items and the red lens blinks when item is being purchased. Simulation ends when all agents exit through the exit gate. Products can be repeated on different shelves to show the idea of going back and forth among different aisles to select and pick the product, where customers encounter the product many times.

There could be many other benefits of using *Swarm-Moves* variations (as described in the chapter about future work). The reorganization of product may be able to gain 5-6% extra sales and the pattern related to customers' path can help us to increase another 4% sales [Xavier 1994]. The RFID enabled shelves can save 6% loss each year because of under-stocking [Xavier 1994]. We believe *Swarm-Sales model* may be extended to find the relationships between groups of products to be offered to customers. There may be no reason for sales of Sponge Bob stuff toy and Harry Potter latest novel together. We want to let the customers make connections, given it is from their average choice. It is evident that humans are very good to make unseen connections as it can be noticed in advertisements like mountains in cigarette publicity and beautiful girls with shaving cream and cars [Lindo 2005].

There could be different layouts for the same simulation. One could prefer multiple entrance and exit gates. One can increase the number of products, categories and/or shelves to have more realistic view of supermarket and one can add multiple race-tracks to it. It all depends on the supermarket you are making the simulation for. The *sales-model* and *swarm-sales model* would be the same for all versions for similar results.

3.6   Items Profile

A profile for each product in the supermarket is stored in a database that is used by the simulator. Each *profile* consists of following 12 parameters: *Item No, Item Name, Price (In US dollar $), Size* (in Cubic Inch), *Weight* (in pounds), *Prominent* *display* (Yes, No), *Life of product* (in days), *On-Sale Off* (How much price is off from cover price, like 10%, 50% etc), *In-Store Advertisement* (what percentage of advertisement displays is holding by that product like 10%, 20% etc), *Bias Value* (one can give value to influence un-observed parameters), *Good Will value* (how much confidence a customer has to use this product), and *Category*.

The customers are more inclined to buy products on impulse from their favorite category. For example, John Doe's favorite category is books and he has 20 extra dollars, there are more chances to buy a latest book of his favorite author on impulse than buying a fishing rod. This behavior is coded through the *likelihood* of buying a product of each category in the *customers' profiles*.

The bias value can serve (although not used in *Swarm-Sales model*) as an extra parameter to cover any new bias or parameter, for example if an item has a free-delivery option, user can influence the probability to buy that product in simulation using bias value. This bias value can be used in the decision of buying an item on impulse and can include the influence for un-observable factors as well. Un-observable factors are those conditions which are really hard to quantify, for example affects of weather or store decoration on customers shopping behavior. One could influence the overall probability through bias value which can increase or reduce the chances of purchase.

A sample of the items profiles (database) is shown in Appendix A.

3.7   Customers' Profile

It is quite intuitive to think that customers have profiles that represent their product preference. Customers may be interested in CDs but not interested in books. The profile of such a customer represents the *likelihood* that (all things being equal) he/she will pick up a product by impulse (not a planned item).

It should be clear that what this profile indicates is that customers have different preferences in relation to products. For instance a customer may be more inclined to by products in c(A), meaning the class of product A, than in c(B), with c(A) ? c(B). By "all things being equal" it is meant that the product A and B have the same characteristics that influence impulse purchase such as price, discount level, etc. Products within the same category are seen as the same product. Although one could implement a simulator with a different degree of granularity for the profiles, for the purposes of showing the effect of the Swarm-Sales model, the categories are sufficient. In order words, one could have a simulator where a Jazz CD is different from a Rap CD, or even the artist can be considered but we argue that this does not affect our results. In a real store, with real customers, the more detailed the profile is the better the decisions can be made.

For the purpose of this simulator the price of the product is being disregarded. This does not make the model unrealistic because one can assume that customers have budgets and will always stay within their budget—they will consider all products within their budget with the same likelihood independent of the products price. In a sense, *Swarm-Sales model* considers only products that are within the customers purchase level. This probability of buying a product on a certain category is influenced by other factors in this work: discount level, and collective sales level.

The customer profile consists of 6 parameters: the number of *planned items* an agents supposed to buy; *Impulse pocket*—the extra money an agent has to buy on impulse (if any); the *size* preference; the *weight* preference; the *decision threshold* (how likely customer is to buy on impulse); and *category [1..n]* (*likelihood* to buy a product from particular category on impulse based on customers personal profile and like and dislike); *decision threshold* is an important factor in making decisions; if the agent has a low threshold, he/she is prone to buy most of the things until he/she ran out of money. If the agent has a high threshold, he/she will be more selective in buying things on impulse, *decision threshold* will be added in future versions of *Swarm-Moves* simulation. Note that these parameters allow the simulator to be more realistic because they allow to code customers with different behavior (common in any supermarket).

Every agent (when see a product) starts with a given *likelihood* to buy this item on impulse, then *Sales-Model* and *Swarm-Sales model* influence this probability to increase it. For example: if the *likelihood* of buying an item is 40% and there is an 80% sale price being offered for that product the overall probability to buy that item will increase (it will become higher than 40%). Similarly, if the 30% of the customers in the supermarket are buying the product, the probability will also increase. The rate of increase is given by the equations that implement the behavior of the models..

The sample of customers' profile is given in Appendix B.

3.8   Programming Assumptions

The simulation has made a few assumptions at the implementation level over the general *Swarm-Sales* model:

- *Agents have enough money to buy planned items therefore the simulation is not calling any function to make a decision on planned items.* The concern about planned items is unnecessary because it is not the focus of this work.

- *Agents can see only one product at a time.* In order to ignore the distraction caused by other products and advertisement in real-life, it is a whole new task to code the *distraction* and the factors that take place it in supermarket. This simulation is sequentially processing every product in customers' line-of-sight and computes its probability to make a decision of purchase.

- *There is no shortage of items in the shelves.* Items are lined up in the queue, as soon as one item sold another is placed on the shelf. This eliminates the need for controlling stock for products. Also, shortages of products in stock can askew the results because customers would not be able to buy it, even after making a decision for its purchase.

- *Information about the content of trolleys can be communicated in real-time.* This means that shopping carts and products are technologically equipped (i.e. RFID, Wi-Fi etc) to enable the store to know what each customer has on its trolley at any point in time.

- *Customer cannot buy same product twice.* As described earlier, this assumption is made to reduce the chances of recommendations in case of extraordinary pattern. For instance, a customer buying 100 knives should not have the same effect as 100 customers buying 1 knife each.

CHAPTER 4

▼

RESULTS

This chapter concentrates on demonstrating that *Swarm-Sales model* is indeed a model able to show improvement on the overall sales volume in supermarkets. Based on what can be seen here in simulations, it is argued that *Swarm-Sales* model is an interesting sales tool. As observed by results presented later, the effects of *Swarm-Sales* model is comparable to the effects of sales prices and price promotions in the supermarket but more importantly the *Swarm-Sales model* offer similar results without losing money on sales deals or price reduction. It is argued that *Swarm-Sales model* is able to generate better unit sales by incorporating *average common choice* as a feedback to other customers.

The following results are average of 2,000 sample runs with different number of agents in each set of simulation (ranging from 200 to 500—experiments used minimum 200 agents to have enough agents to calculate the *average common choice* and maximum 500 agents due to the limited supply of unique *customer profiles*). Products and agents details were loaded from their respective profiles, and no random value (i.e. value for *likelihood, favorite* category, *product price* etc) has been selected during the simulation. The samples of items and agents profiles are given in Appendices *A* and *B*.

Figures 4.1 clearly demonstrate the performance of *swarm-sales model* over *customer profiles* and *sales model. Swarm-Sales* model is able to get more than double sales over *customer profiles* and 29% extra over *sales model*. The total average sales of supermarket with 200 agents with *customers profile* is US$ 61,329, and US$ 104,033 while incorporating the *sales model* into it, and it increases to total sales of US$ 130,765 with *swarm-sales model*.

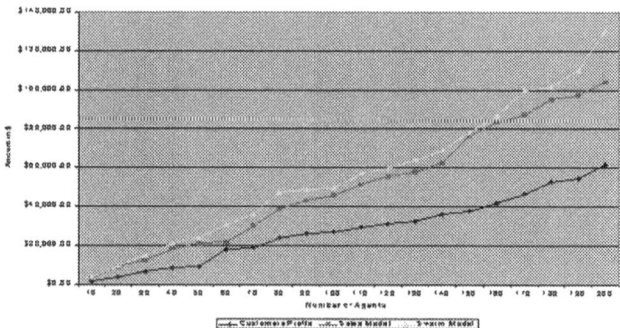

Figure 4.1: Total Sales based on Customer Profiles, Sales and Swarm-Sales model

In Figure 4.2 one can see the effect of *swarm-sales model* on overall sales which looks like the sigmoid; this is not surprising, due to the use of sigmoid based equation in the model that comes from the general findings on people's responses under different settings as described in Section 3.1. There is a threshold point (30% sales) in graph which changes the customer's decision to buy the product and at certain point (80% sales) it will stabilize. This threshold and stabilization point can be different for each product of different categories.

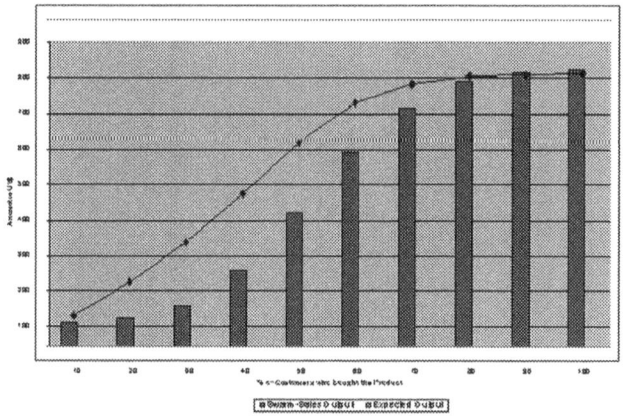

Figure 4.2: Expected Vs Actual output of Swarm-Sales Model

Swarm-Moves simulation is used to run experiments with *Swarm-Sales model* and *Sales Model* to find out the optimum percentage of average promotion-depth in the supermarket. The optimum number of agents for the sample runs is found to be 200 (after empirical analysis)—because few number of agents has produced negligible difference in profit and loss margin, while large number of agents has only increased the intensity of profit and loss margin with the same optimum points. The values of parameters in *sales model* and *swarm-sales model* being used are the same as described earlier in Section 3.1. The charts depicted in Figures 4.4 and 4.5 demonstrate a loss in profit after the depth in promotion (percentage off from regular price) reaches 50%, since the average profit margin is 50% in the supermarket (this value is coming from the items profiles—product actual and label price to calculate the profit).

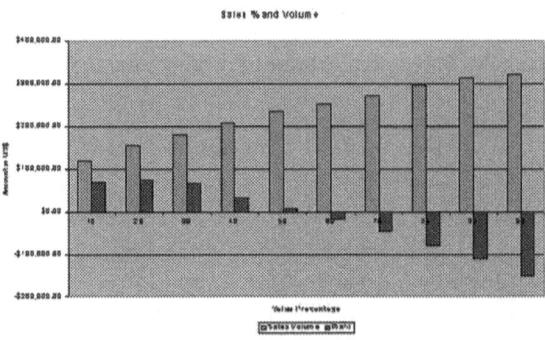

Figure 4.3: Optimum Percentage of Depth-of-Promotion in *Sales-Model*

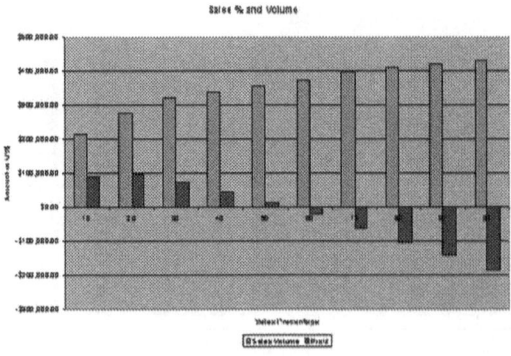

Figure 4.4: Optimum Percentage of Depth-of-Promotion in *Swarm-Sales model*

20% *average sales-off* price has achieved the highest profit and 50% *average sales-off* price has achieved the highest sales-volume in both models in the supermarket.

As observed in this simulation, if the supermarket wants the highest profit, the average depth of promotion can go up to 20%. If the highest sales-volume is the priority, the average depth of promotion can go up to 50%. The average profit (price—cost) of all products in the supermarket is the key to decide what maximum percentage of depth of promotion a supermarket can or should offer to its customers. This experiment should be run with supermarkets real data to have a customized recommendation for individual supermarkets—results shown here are just an example of how to benefit from this simulation.

There is no difference in optimum points of promotion depth in *sales* or *swarm-sales* model; however, the effect is more intense in case of *swarm-sales model*. For instance, the maximum profit made by *swarm-sales model* is US$ 94,919 versus US$ 75,606 maximum profit made by *sales model*, similarly the maximum loss made by *swarm-sales model* is US$ 185,053 versus US$ 150,098 incase of *sales model*.

Another experiment is carried out to find out the average spending of customers in the supermarket through *Swarm-Moves* simulation while using different models (*customer profiles, sales-model* and *swarm-sales model*). The experiment results are shown in Figure 4.5, the values are taken from the average of 200 runs. The *Swarm-Sales model* has the highest average customer spending in the supermarket, more than double the average spending of *customers' profile* and 29% extras as compared to *Sales-Model*.

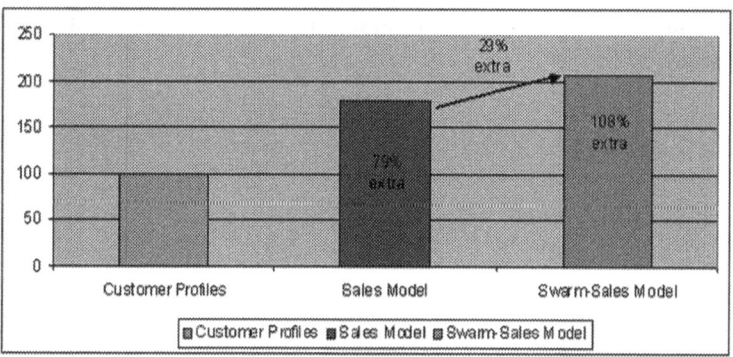

Figure 4.5: Average Customer Spending in the Supermarket

A few more experiments have been carried out to know the effect of number of customers (sensitivity analysis) on average spending in the supermarket. The *customer profiles* and *sales model* cause the similar up-and-down effect on average customers' spending in the supermarket. In both cases (*customer profiles* and *sales-model*) customers are not interacting with each other (except they can see what others are buying in moving trolleys in a real supermarket). One of the reasons of fluctuations in average spending in case of *customer profiles* and *sales model* is the lack of coordination among customers—customers are not connected or communicated to each other by any means and causing a random pattern.

Swarm-Sales model as expected had shown a clear linearly increasing graph of average spending directly proportional to the number of agents in the supermarket. The more agents you have in the supermarket, the more average spending per customer you will get (if the supermarket is using the *Swarm-Sales model*). The average spending of customers in case of total 10 customers in the market increases as high as 77% in case of 200 customers in the supermarket. The more customers you get the more influence you will create to buy on impulse or follow the crowd.

The 29% increase in impulse shopping using *Swarm-Sales model* over *Sales-Model* is a significant improvement. *Swarm-Moves* is providing a platform to test different variables with different values (i.e. no of customers, products etc). There is no *Optimum Stage* (when we can say that all stakeholders are 100% satisfied) in this process, since all recommendations are based on current customers. There could be all different set of recommendations and settings for next few hours depending on the customers and what they are buying. There could be different settings according to density of particular group in the supermarket like children, teenagers or senior citizens. Overall, to influence customers to buy more on impulse is proved to be a good technique for supermarket optimization and to increase sales.

CHAPTER 5

▼

CONCLUSION & FUTURE WORK

The thesis proposed the *Swarm-Sales Model* to increase sales in supermarkets and introduced a simulation called *Swarm-Moves* to validate the proposed model. The simulation offers an effective marketing tool to current stores to increase their sales volume based on emergent properties of customers in the store. As of today, *Swarm-Moves* can answer many questions such as: What is the relationship between depth of promotion and sales-volume? What is the collective customers' choice in a given amount of time? And what is the average spending of customers in a supermarket given we have total number of customers and the total amount of their respective purchases?

Overall, the research has demonstrated the power of collective information in sales optimization—*Swarm-Moves* simulation along with its model to influence impulse shopping is a new direction in supermarket optimization. It offers an effective marketing tool for current supermarkets to increase sales and profits in supermarkets. Additionally, as a marketing tool, one could argue that the *Swarm-Sales* model is likely to provide a better customer satisfaction because they get the impression that the store is providing useful information about the status of what are the "good deals" at any point in time. Not to say that the information is not useful, but as described here, it is a customer satisfaction tool as a side-effect of the main process which is the increase of sales.

This research could have a significant impact in future supermarkets that will be equipped with the latest technologies that can pass the customers' purchases information in real-time (e.g. RFID, Wi-Fi) and *Swarm-Sales model* can exploit this data to make the supermarket more profitable.

Swarm-Sales model can help the understanding of customers' patterns and the influence of impulse shopping in supermarkets. In the test case *Swarm-Sales model* has improved the real time impulse shopping in simulation by 29%.

The results in this thesis indicate that environmental information can be used to influence customers to purchase more on impulse. However should be validated in a real supermarket setting. This has not been performed due to the difficulties in convincing the supermarket to let one look at their everyday process of deciding prices, promotions, etc. as they all consider their own process as confidential. Despite the difficulties in getting a supermarket to test the approach we are looking into how to validate *Swarm-Sales model* with real stores and real customers. Given the simulated results, it may be easier to approach the stores so they can see that they are likely to gain something from this study.

In the future the *Swarm-Moves* could be extended to answer many other questions that could also help retail stores on their decision making process:

1. *What is the effect of products' individual factors on impulse shopping?* One could start by adding other influencing factors for impulse shopping (like size, life of the product, brand, advertisement, prominent display, bargains etc) in the equation to see the impact of individual factor and its value over the total impulse shopping. This will help managers to market the product efficiently by using the best possible way.

2. *What is the most prominent factor to increase impulse shopping in real-time?* One can start by examining the relationship of in-store factors to overall sales volume, for instance, what level of advertisement is necessary to promote the new product or what percentage of extra sales a supermarket can get by placing a product on prominent displays? Can mass distribution of product with advertisement cause the same effects as of bargains? There are a number of questions on the same line that could be answered following this direction for future work. Few of these parameters are already given in *Swarm-Moves* simulation screen to work on. These questions are necessary and required for better marketing and promotion of the product, thus increasing impulse shopping in the supermarkets.

3. *Should we impose 'cross categorization' to increase sales in a given time? Or should we impose 'uniform categorization'* to help the customer to find a product and to save time. Another dimension to be benefited from the *Swarm-Moves* simulation is to program and test different layouts and settings for the supermarket and find out the optimum design.

4. *What is the most common path of customers?* One could start analyzing the actual paths customers are taking to find out the congested routes or the locations suitable for prominent displays. This could be helpful to design more customer-friendly supermarkets by providing more race-tracks or less congested routes.

5. *What would be the effect of adding shelves and/or product in sales of supermarket?* It is related to the question above; one could also add and remove shelves from the simulation to examine its effects on overall sales. This could be helpful in designing and maintaining the supermarkets for more sales and optimal output.

There are several improvements that can be made in the future. First, the simulation does not act on all customers at the same level. With one entrance and less initial data (as happening in the current version of simulation) the recommendations traveled through old to new customers in the supermarket. For example, customers who first enter in the supermarket have least benefits (all new recommendations are for late customers who can get the feedback of early customers). This problem can be solved by using parallel layout or multiple entrances and exits by providing uniform feedback (everyone gets the same feedback).

A controversial parameter is on-sale; if we place the products on sale in real-time, customers can have different prices of the same product bought from the same store in a same day. One would like to work on offering bargains of two or more things together which becomes the average common choice of customers in the supermarket—that is the number of instances of purchasing same items together by different customers.

There is another dimension to look at the benefits of *Swarm-Sales model*. It may be used to help customers to make more educated and profitable (from customers' perspective) decisions. While at the one end supermarket may lose small amount of sales, it can get the customers' loyalty and satisfied (thus returning) customers because of good shopping experience. Research needs to be done to measure customer satisfaction after deployment of *Swarm-Sales* model. It is evident that customer satisfaction always yields more profit and sales to the store (since loyal customers are more tolerant to buy on higher prices) [Kumar 2006].

The measurement of customer satisfaction would be a good start for the extension of this work. Quite a lot of research has been done on the definition of customers' satisfaction parameters and the uniqueness of these parameters for each customer. Some researchers argue that customer satisfaction is mainly based on quality of product, which has two basic parameters: fitness (is the product doing what is supposed to do?) and reliability [Berthiaume 2004]. Other factors related to customer satisfaction include: speed of shopping, values of money, price, and bargain as core parameters of customers' satisfaction [Ma 2005]. It is an open question of the effectiveness of *Swarm-Moves* on the answering of these questions, but with more research, some of these may be included in the simulation.

REFERENCES

[**AWM 2005**] Arc Worldwide Magazine, *Why they buy what they buy: Understanding shopping behavior.* Specs. In A chain store age event, 2005

[**Bangoli 1987**] Judann Bangoli. *Impulse governs shoppers.* Advertising Age, pages 2–3, 1987.

[**Berger 2000**] Arthur Asa Berger. *Ads, Fads and Consumer Culture.* Rowman & Littlefield Publishers, 2000.

[**Berthiaume 2004**] Dan Berthiaume, *RFID Boost Customer Satisfaction at TESCO*, Retail Technology Quarterly, January 2004

[**Bonabeau 1999**] E. Bonabeau, M. Dorigo, and G. Theraulaz. *Swarm Intelligence: From Natural to Artificial Systems.* Santa Fe Institute Studies in the Sciences of Complexity Series. Oxford Press, July 1999.

[**Bonabeau 2001**] E. Bonabeau and C. Meyer. *Swarm intelligence: A whole new way to think about business.* Harvard Business Review, 79(5):106–114, May 2001.

[**Bonabeau 2002**] Eric Bonabeau, *Agent-based modeling: Methods and techniques for simulating human systems.* Proceedings of the National Academy of Sciences, 99(Supplement 3): 7280–7287, May 2002.

[**Bucklin 2001**] Randolph E Bucklin, David R Bell and Catarina Sismeiro. *Consumer shopping behaviors and in-store expenditure decisions.* In Consumer Shopping Behaviors, 2001.

[**Costjens 1981**] Marcel Corstjens and Peter Doyle. *A model for optimizing retail space allocations.* 1981.

[**Cotton 1978**] B. C. Cotton. *Consumer Response to Promotional Deals.* Journal of Marketing, July 14th 1978.

[**Cox 1970**] Keith K. Cox. *The effect of shelf space upon sales of branded products.* Journal of Marketing Research, I:55–59, 1970.

[**Curhan 1972**] Ronald C. Curhan. *The relationship between shelf space and unit sales in supermarkets.* Journal of Marketing Research, IX:406–412, 1972.

[**Danziger 2004**] Pamela N. Danziger. *Why People Buy Things They Don't Need.* Paramount Market Publishing, 2004.

[**Dawes 2004**] John Dawes. *Accessing the impact of a very successful price promotion on brand, category and competitor sales.* The journal of product and brand management, 2004, 13, 4/5

[**Dologite 1993**] Dorothy G. Dologite. *Developing a knowledge-based system for product position advertising strategy formulation.* IEEE, 0-18186-3730-7, 1993.

[**Duncan 2001**] Eric Duncan. *Long-Run Effects of Promotion Depth on New Versus Established Customers: Three field studies.* 2001

[**Edward 1995**] Robert Edward. *How Promotion Works.* Marketing Science, summer 1995, 14, 3.

[**Garrick 1986**] G Garrick. *Spend better advertising dollars, not more.* Advertising Research Foundation, Electronic Media Workshop, 1986.

[**Hoch 1989**] Stephen. J. Hoch and John. Deighton. *Managing what consumers learn from experience.* Journal of Marketing, 53:1–20, 1989.

[**Jacoby 2002**] Jacob Jacoby. *Stimulus-organism-response reconsidered: An evolutionary step in modeling (consumer) behavior.* Journal of Consumer Psychology, 12(1):51–57, 2002.

[**Jadedi 1999**] Kamel Jedidi, Carl. F. Mela, Sunil Gupta. *Managing Advertising and Promotion for long run profitability.* Marketing Science, 1999. 18, 1.

[**Jhonson 2004**] M. Eric Jhonson, David F. Pyke. *Real time profit optimization: Coordinating demand and supply chain management.* 2004.

[**Kennedy 2001**] James Kennedy and Russell C Eberhart. *Swarm Intelligence.* Morgan Kaufman Publishers, 2001.

[**Kumar 2006**] V. Kumar, Rajkumar Venkatesan and Werner Reinartz, *Knowing What to sell, When and to Whom,* Harvard Business Review, pp 131–137, March 2006

[**Larson 2004**] Jeffrey S. Larson. *An exploratory look at supermarket shopping paths.* 2004.

[**Lee 2004**] Grant Lee. *Wal-militia: The Conspiracy of Wal-Mart and the Government : A National Report.* Xlibris Corporation, 2004.

[**LINDO 2005**] Lindo Systems. *Applications of Optimization to Problems in Sales and Marketing.* Lindo Systems, 2005.

[**Ma 2005**] Li Ma *et al.,* Customer Satisfaction and Service and System Based on Motive—Hygiene Theory, ICEC'05, August 15-17 2005

[**Marks 1998**] Robert E. Marks, G. M. Shiraz. *Using genetic algorithms to breed competitive marketing strategies.* 1998.

[**Milliman 1982**] Ronald E. Milliman. *Using background music to affect the behavior of supermarket shoppers.* Journal of Marketing, I:86–91, 1982.

[**Morrison 1999**] Michael Morrison. *The power of music and its influence on international retail brands and shopper behavior: A multi case study approach.*

Monash University, 1999.

[**Naert 1988**] Philippe Naert, Alain Bultez. *SHARP: Shelf allocation for retailers' profit. Marketing Science,* 7, 1988.

[**Nagle 1987**] Thomas T. Nagle. *The Strategy of Pricing.* Prentice Hall, 1987.

[**Neilson 1992**] A. C. Neilson Tej anand, Gary Kahn. *Focusing knowledge based techniques on market analysis.* 1992.

[**Newman 1999**] Bruce I. Newman, Jagdish N. Sheth, Banwari Mittal. *CustomerBehavior-Consumer Behavior and Beyond.* The Dryden Press, 1999.

[**Reinhold 1983**] Health Safety and Human Factors Laboratory. *Ergonomic Design for People at Work Vol-I & II.* Van Nostrand Reinhold—New York, 1983.

[**Rheingold 2002**] Howard Rheingold. *Smart Mobs-The Next Social Revolution.* Perseus Publishing, 2002.

[**Rosen 2002**] Emanuel Rosen. *The Anatomy of Buzz: How to Create Word of Mouth Marketing.* Currency Publishers, 2002.

[**Rousseeuw 2005**] Peter J. Rousseeuw Leonard Kaufman. *Finding Groups in Data: An Introduction to Cluster Analysis.* Addison Wesley, 2005.

[**Salzman 2003**] Marian Salzman. *Buzz: Harness the Power of Influence and Create Demand.* Wiley, 2003.

[**Smith 1989**] Daniel C. Smith, C. Whan Park, Easwar S. Iyer. *The effects of situational factors on in-store grocery shopping behavior: The role of store environment and time available for shopping.* Journal of Consumer Research, 15:422—433, 1989.

[**Sommer 1982**] Robert Sommer and Susan Aitkens. *Mental mapping of two supermarkets.* The Journal of Consumer Research, 9:211–215, 1982.

[**Stern 1962**] Hawkins Stern. *The significance of impulse buying today.* Nature and Significance of Consumer Impulse Buying, I:59–62, 1962.

[**Supermarket 2003**] Supermarket Research. *Supermarket strategic alert special report,*

[**Thiesing 1997**] *Frank M. Thiesing and Oliver Vornberger. Sales forecasting using neural networks.* IEEE 0-7803-4122-8/97, pages 2125–2128, 1997.

[**UIE 2001**] User Interface Engineering. *What causes customers to buy on impulse?* E-Commerce White paper, I:1—10, 2001.

[**V Kumar 2006**] V. Kumar *et al.,* Knowing What to Sell, When and to Whom, HBR, March 2006

[**Vornberger 1994**] Oliver Vornberger, Frank M. Thiesing, Ulrich Middleberg. *Short term prediction of sales in supermarkets.* University of Osnabruck, Germany, 1994.

[**Vornberger 1997**] Oliver Vornberger, Frank M. Thiesing. *Sales forecasting using neural networks.* IEEE, 1997.

[**Williamson 1999**] Michael Williamson. *Point-of-purchase display and brand sales.* In Casio Electronics Ltd, 1999.

[**Xavier 1994**] Mary E. Purk Xavier Dreze, Stephen J. Hoch. *Shelf management and space elasticity.* 1994.

[**Zaltman 2003**] Gerald Zaltman. *How Customers Think-Essential Insights into the Mind of the Market.* Harvard Business School Press, 2003.

APPENDIX A: SAMPLE ITEM PROFILES

Item#	Item Name	Price	Size	Adv	Prominent	Weight	Life	OnSale-Off	Category	Bias	GoodWill
1	File Folder	4	61	0	1	610	61	0.6	1	0	0
2	Ball Points	10	62	0	0	620	62	0	1	0	0
3	Stapler	5	63	0	0	630	63	0.6	1	0	0
4	Whole Punch	20	64	0	0	640	64	0.6	1	0	0
5	Schrader	110	65	0	1	650	65	0.6	1	0	0
6	Paper Rim	22	66	0	0	660	66	0.6	1	0	0
7	Pencil	4	67	0	0	670	67	0	1	0	0
8	Colors	4	68	0	0	680	68	0	1	0	0
9	Marker	3	69	0	0	690	69	0	1	0	0.5
10	Gum Stick	6	70	0	0	700	70	0	1	0	0.5
11	CD Player	50	1	0	1	10	1	0	2	0	0.1
12	DVD Player	40	2	0	1	20	2	0.1	2	0	0.2
13	VCR	40	3	0	0	30	3	0.15	2	0	0.3
14	Audio Recorder	10	4	0	0	40	4	0.2	2	0	0.4
15	USB Drive	60	5	0	0	50	5	0	2	0	0.5

APPENDIX B: SAMPLE AGENT PROFILES

Agent #	Planned Items	Pocket	Size	Weight	Cat1	Cat2	Cat3	Cat4	Cat5	Cat6	Cat7	Cat8	Cat9	Cat10	Cat11	Cat12	Dec-Th
1	10	1500	10	10	0.12	0.11	0.09	0	0	0	0	0	0	0.013	0.658	0.001	0.1
2	9	600	5	20	0.02	0.02	0.02	0.02	0.01	0.01	0.01	0.01	0.01	0.005	0.868	0.002	0.2
3	8	500	5	30	0	0	0.01	0.01	0.01	0.01	0.01	0.01	0.02	0.88	0.019	0.021	0.3
4	7	400	5	40	0	0.01	0.01	0	0	0.01	0.01	0.02	0.93	0.009	0.004	0.002	0.4
5	6	300	3	50	0.01	0.01	0.01	0	0.03	0.01	0.08	0.76	0.01	0.084	0.003	0.002	0.5
6	5	200	2	60	0.01	0.01	0.01	0	0	0.01	0.92	0.02	0.01	0.009	0.004	0.002	0.6
7	4	100	1	70	0.01	0.01	0.01	0	0	0.84	0.09	0.01	0.01	0.008	0.003	0.002	0.7

978-0-595-43848-8
0-595-43848-2